It is
ALL
POSSIBLE
for you

15 steps for taking control of your journey

Duncan Woods

It is ALL POSSIBLE for you © 2018
Written by, Duncan Woods
Illustrations by, Samuel Müller

ISBN: 9781793099518

Dedication

This book is dedicated to the spirit of Madiba.

You have shown us that it is ALL possible if we can learn to love, and dare to keep growing even when all hope seems lost.

"It always seems impossible until it is done."

-Nelson Rolihlahla Mandela (1918-2013)

A note from the Author

"I have been fortunate enough to locate a core passion in trying to help people live their lives with deep awareness and strong purpose. This is a short collection of personal lessons that I believe can help in that process.

This book is about growth, and in many ways has been an important part of my own growth. Much of the content is messages that I am writing equally for my own awareness, as much as that of the reader.

May we all have the courage to keep growing and learning. And never losing sight that we are truly able to create the life we deeply desire."

Duncan Woods

December 2018

A note from the Illustrator

"From a young age, my two main passions have been found in sport and drawing. I have played football for many years and have always enjoyed sketching in my free time.

At the moment, I am in the process of trying to make one of my passions my career by studying illustration as part of my education in design.

I hope this book will inspire people to live their lives more confidently. Personally, thinking about how to illustrate the messages in the different chapters certainly helped me grow as a person."

Samuel Muller

December 2018

SAMUEL MULLER IS A YOUNG AND TALENTED ARTIST AND ILLUSTRATOR BASED IN HERZOGENAURACH, GERMANY.

TO VIEW HIS GROWING PORTFOLIO OF PLEASE VISIT:
SAMUHERZO.MYPORTFOLIO.COM

Contents

How To Make This Book Most Useful For You

When you consider how many fantastic and insightful books you have read over the years, it is a shame that you probably can only recall a handful of their more powerful messages.

With this in mind, I would like to encourage you to approach this book in a way that will maximize its usefulness.

The approach I recommend is as follows:

1. Read the book from cover to cover making shorthand notes and underlining the points that have an impact on you. (I believe the book is concise enough to read in one sitting.)

2. Once complete, go back through each chapter from beginning to end, and reflect specifically on each of Youme's challenges to you.

3. Have a paper or digital notepad at the ready to journal the learnings that you take from the lessons.

4. Make notes reflecting how this lesson can be put into action to start taking control of your personal journey.

Through this journaling process, let your spontaneity flow and write down whatever comes to you in that moment. The sub-conscious mind is a treasure trove of insights for us, so just let the words flow. You may be surprised with how much emerges when we start actively self-reflecting.

5. Some lessons will have more personal impact than others, so I recommend you spend the most time on those that produce the most thoughts and reflections for you. However, I would encourage you to note some thoughts on each lesson. Often the most important personal topics are the ones that we try and hide from or avoid. Be brave enough to address the difficult topics.

6. Over the longer term, keep this book handy, on your desktop or next to your bedside. Paging through the lessons from time to time will keep the messages fresh and the personal journey alive

INTRODUCTION

This is Youme

Youme has spent his entire time on earth riding the ups and downs of life. There were days when Youme was on top of the world. There were also days when Youme wanted to hide under the bedcovers.

As Youme moved from being a boy to becoming a man, he started to wonder if there was something going on behind the scenes.

These wonderings were at first very hushed, but as the candles on his birthday cake began to gather in a crowd, the whispers became more of a beating bass drum, and he could not stop tapping his feet to the rhythm.

Youme realized he was beginning to see a pattern behind the game of life. He saw that we can control how we think and how we live. Youme found this fantastically interesting and spreading the news of the pattern became the most interesting thing in the world to him.

So, one day he got off the bus, and started walking around, following his own path.

He discovered we all get to decide what is possible.

And it IS all possible for Youme. And for you. And for me.

Here are a few lessons he has picked up along the way and wants to share with you

CHAPTER ONE:

GO WITH THE HEART

Youme believes you should: "Lead with the heart."

There will be those who are talented and there will be those who are smart. There will also be those that are both talented and smart. But it is the people with heart that are the ones that you know will be fighting to the end. Feast or famine, losing or winning, you know they will be the ones holding up the flag until the end.

Use your body and you can become strong.

Use your mind and you can become smart.

Use your heart and you cannot be stopped.

Take note of the things your heart pulls you towards and follow them. That is where your deepest strength lies.

"Your mind and body can both be beaten, but your heart is undefeatable. Lead with your heart and you will be unstoppable."

- Bryant McGill

6

Youme challenge:

Which kind of person would you like to be known as?

· The talented one?

· The smart one?

· The one who lived with all their heart?

Now, feel what it is your heart is calling you to follow?

GO WITH THE HEART

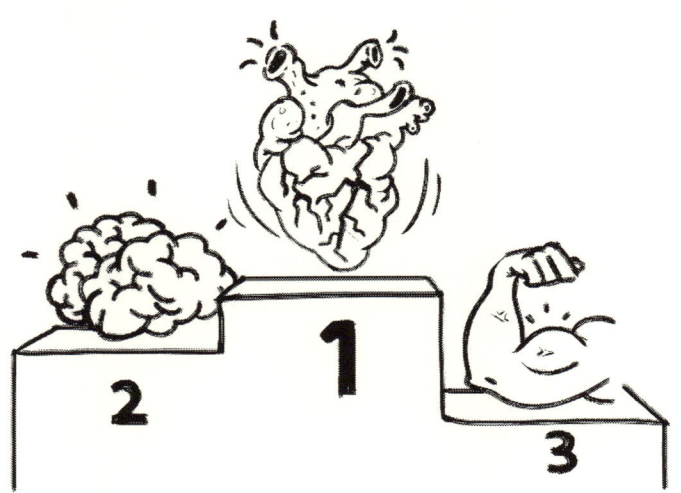

CHAPTER TWO:

JUST BE YOURSELF

Youme says: "Just be yourself."

You damn magnificent thing, when are you going to realize you are your own unique selling point?

- *You are the only one that can DO you.*

- *You are the only one that can BE you.*

No one could ever offer what you have to offer. Society requires structure and so will try and box you into a category or description. Your competitive advantage lies in your special experience and the unique accumulation of your life learnings, which cannot be replicated.

"To be beautiful means to be yourself. You don't need to be accepted by others. You need to accept yourself."

- Thich-Nhat Hanh

Youme challenge:

No one else knows, nor will ever know, the notes to your tune.

So, find your own tune and play it. That is what sets you apart.

So, if your life had a theme song, what would it be?

I WANT YOU TO
BE YOURSELF

CHAPTER THREE:

GET OUT OF YOUR OWN WAY

Youme says: "Get out of your own way."

A pendulum moves with a beautiful fluidity and effortless rhythm through its range. The freedom of movement is mesmerising to watch. But any obstruction dramatically alters that flow. The movements become restricted, jerky and limited. The new intensity of movement now becomes *hard* to watch.

So, think of the rhythm of your life like the pendulum. Think which movement you would like to live out...the effortless rhythm...OR... the jerky and troubled?

Now, challenge yourself to stop being the obstacle in your own way. Decide what you want your life-rhythm to look like. Ignore the doubts and live out your passions with great heart and great courage.

"Doubt kills more dreams than failure ever will."

- Suzy Kassem

Youme challenge:

Where are you getting in your own way?

· Take note where YOU are the blockage…

· Why is that?

· Is there any good to come from blocking your own progress?

You decide…and then commit to getting out the way!!!

GET OUT OF YOUR OWN WAY

CHAPTER FOUR:

DECIDE WHAT YOU ARE LIVING FOR

Youme asks: "What are you living for?"

In the expanse of time, we are on the Earth for just a fleeting moment.

What you are living out today, another day at work or play, will be insignificant in a month, a year, or a decade's time.

So, what is it that you can do that will making an enduring impression on the world?

It will likely not be anything you do for yourself. Those things will disappear with you. What bigger cause can you grow and move forward with your time?

"Society grows great when old men plant trees under whose shade they know they will never sit."

- Greek proverb.

Youme challenge:

Everyone has the opportunity to leave a legacy…

So, what would you like yours to be?

What are the "footprints" that you want to leave behind as you walk through life?

Take some time and describe what you would like to leave behind on Earth.

WHAT AM I LIVING FOR ?

CHAPTER FIVE:

DEFINE WHAT YOU ARE TRYING TO CREATE

Youme asks: "What does a successful life look like for you?"

We all want to be successful. But we need to understand that success is different for everyone.

Our culture projects that success is measured in terms of wealth. But, don't be fooled into thinking that is the only way to be successful. This would be a hugely limiting assumption. We cannot all be wealthy in financial terms, so why do we allow ourselves to be limited to this measure?

"I know some people who are so poor; all they have is money".

- Gaur Gopal Das

...And you don't need to look very far to see many wealthy and "successful" people battling with conflict, turmoil, and emptiness, elsewhere in their lives.

You are worth more than your job. Do not let that define your success. Look deeper. Dare to be brave with your version of success.

<u>Youme challenge:</u>

So, a really important question to ask yourself: "What does a successful life look like for me?"

Make your list now for each part of your life:

· In your work

· With your partner

· With your parents

· With your children

· With your friends

· With your health

· Emotionally

· Spiritually

· In the community

· What other areas is it important for me to define success...?

WHAT DOES SUCCESS LOOK LIKE?

CHAPTER SIX:

KNOW WHO YOU NEED TO BE

Youme reminder: "You get to choose who shows up."

Every day, in every situation, you get to decide which version of yourself shows up.

Every golf shot requires a different club. Same person. Same swing. But, a very different approach is needed to shape the moment.

Your life is, in many ways, the same. We need to match the energy that we bring with us to be appropriate to the situation. The version of yourself that shows up to deliver the big work presentation, is not the same person you need to be when you are cuddling your children or when you are dealing with a major trauma.

Youme encourages you to begin to develop your understanding of the range of energies that you can bring to life. Get to know the different energies you bring and put them to work to get the most out of each situation. Understand who you are capable of being in different moments, and how that awareness can help shape the outcome you want.

"Showing up is essential. Showing up consistently is powerful. Showing up consistently with a positive outlook is even more powerful."

- Jeff Olsen

Youme challenge:

In your next big (and small) moments, decide who you need to be and step into it.

· Before arriving at a meeting or social engagement, decide which version of yourself is showing up: the serious, focused and efficient; or the bubbly and enthusiastic part of you? Yes!!! You get to choose...

· Now can you own that for one day? Then two? Then three? Then a week?

WHO DO I NEED TO BE NOW ?

CHAPTER SEVEN:

UNDERSTAND YOUR PERSONAL POWER

Youme wants you to consider: "The Power Equation"

In every situation you have a choice...

Am I going to stand in my power? Or am I going to give my power to someone else?

"No one can make you feel inferior without your consent."

- Eleanor Roosevelt

When you face something that really challenges you to your core, perhaps you have just lost the big match, the big sales pitch, when that thing you really wanted is just not happening...think carefully about what you do with your personal power. Allowing yourself to be overcome by disappointment and despair gives all the power to the situation or the other person and the longer it goes on, the harder it becomes to bounce back.

So, what does keeping the power look like?

Stand tall in your shoes and resolve to keep learning and growing. Take each setback as merely a bump in the road on the way to fulfilment. Despite the loss, no one can stop you from bouncing back... *IF* you keep holding the power. Decide what the next definite forward step can be and go there.

Choose to be the person you want to be and stand in your power in every moment.

Youme challenge:

In what situations have you given your power to another?

· How can you learn from that?

· How can you take that power back?

· What is the definitive and productive next step?

THE POWER EQUATION

or

CHAPTER EIGHT:

MANAGE YOUR SELF-TALK

Youme wants you to learn to manage your own thoughts

In the build-up to any situation with deep meaning for you, the big speech, the big exam, the collaboration that could change it all, the interview for the dream job; we need to be really strong in managing the words we tell ourselves.

As you go about your preparation actively start analysing your thoughts. Is this thought "lifting me up" or is it "pushing me down"?

Your thoughts become things, and you can think yourself into being outstanding, or you can think yourself out of being outstanding. It is literally yours to create.

Train your mind to make sure you are only filling up the positive box and starving the negative box.

Like the Cherokee Indian story of the two wolves. The good wolf; and the evil wolf. The one who wins is the one you feed the most.

"The most important words you hear in your life are the words you tell yourself, about yourself."

- Lisa McInnes-Smith

<u>Youme challenge:</u>

Use this tool to prepare yourself for your next big challenge.

As you start preparing, ask yourself constantly which box you are filling with your thoughts.

· Is this train of thought going to lift me up?

· Or is this thought going to put me down?

It is that simple. Your thoughts are either helping or hurting your preparation.

WHICH BOX ARE YOU CHOOSING ?

CHAPTER NINE:

RUN YOUR OWN RACE

Youme asks: "Where are you moving from?"

Understand that we are all running our own race.

Everyone's race has a unique start and will have a unique finish. The habit of constantly comparing ourselves to others stops being useful when we depart from our unique circumstances and start mimicking the journey of others.

So, start by taking stock of where you are right now.

- What has got you to where you are?

- How long will you stay here?

- What is pushing you from here? Where does the drive and inspiration to move your life forward come from?

- And what lies ahead?

Really absorbing the nature of our unique journey, understanding how you got here, why you got here, and embracing that uniqueness is the very fuel to drive for your future growth.

"If you don't know which port you are sailing to,
then no wind is favourable."

- Unknown

Youme challenge:

· Take a look back on the last few years (or several years if you prefer).

· Take note of how much you have achieved and overcome.

· If you can have done all this, achieved so much, overcome such challenges then surely you have proven to yourself that you have deep resources that are available within you?

· Now, spend some moments visualising the great things that remain to be achieved. Write them down.

RUN YOUR OWN RACE

CHAPTER TEN:

GETTING YOUR PROBLEMS INTO PERSPECTIVE

Youme encourages you to imagine "The Problems Pile"

We all have our worries, fears, problems. But how serious a problem are they *really*?

When you step back and take a look around you at what other people are dealing with, things often take on a new perspective. Open your eyes to see what others are dealing with, and then look back in reflection on what your pile of problems really are.

And prepare to be humbled...because more often than not, we would gladly take our own pile of issues back in a heartbeat.

So, feel blessed.

Be grateful for what you have.

Take a look at all the good things you have in your life.

Take a deep breath, change your attitude and your approach, and get solving.

"We cannot solve our problems with the same thinking we used when we created them."

- Albert Einstein

Youme challenge:

· Write down the 5 things that are worrying you the most right now.

· Next to each, write down the first step you can do to start improving that situation.

All it takes is a fresh perspective and one step or action in a positive direction to start changing the picture.

PROBLEMS PILE

CHAPTER ELEVEN:

GET TO THE ROOT OF THE PROBLEM

Youme says: "If you want to bring about change, go to the root perspective."

Why is it that we cannot shake off the same recurring patterns in our lives? The same themes that keep repeating...the lack of confidence socially or at work, the struggle to find the right relationships, or the perpetual struggle to shed those extra few pounds...

The secret lies in changing the channel at the source. Unplug the television at the wall. Leave the mobile phone in the kitchen. Leave the soft drinks out of the shopping trolley...

The changes you want to see in your life can best be implemented by going down to the roots. Stop messing around on the symptoms. Look beyond the flower and leaves providing a canopy for the problem and go deeper to get to the root cause that is driving the behaviour. Go deep and change the pattern at the roots.

Want a better relationship? How much effort are you investing in actually making it better?

Want a better job? How many extra hours are you putting in to turn "good" work into "great" work?

How much effort are you putting into up-skilling yourself? Great work gets noticed. Good work is expected.

Want more wealth? How much effort are you spending learning about how to be smarter with your money?

Want to lose those extra pounds? Decide what your picture of health looks like and stop wasting time calculating calories.

When you want change, go to the root perspective to make it happen.

"When solving problems, dig at the roots instead of just hacking at the leaves."

- Anthony J. D'Angelo

Youme challenge:

·   What is the one habit that you would like to change?

·   Forget the symptoms, find the root of the problem.

·   Now, find the trigger that starts the process, and put all your efforts into changing your behaviour at that point.

Create the change now. Today.

"Do I really want this?" and "Why do I really want this?" are both powerful questions that can help you stay true to making the sustainable changes you want to see.

HOW TO CHANGE THE CHANNEL

CHAPTER TWELVE:

DECIDE WHAT IS NOT FOR YOU

Youme asks: "What is NOT for you?"

It is so easy to scroll through the glossy social media newsfeed and believe that everyone else has it all figured out. A sign of our time…heavily filtered images of our friends absolutely 'nailing it' on Instagram, but in reality, all of us are wrestling with some real challenges in the quiet of our lives.

Do yourself a favour and understand that the doctored and picture-perfect family images are only a highlights reel. It is so easy to get seduced into believing that you are missing out somewhere or that others have somehow 'got the drop' on you.

"Life is the most difficult exam. Many people fail because they try to copy others, not realising that everyone has a different question paper."

-Unknown

On this life journey we are all required to live both the highlights and the lowlights. Without the lows, we wouldn't know the highs. Each of us has as much or as little in our life as what we have made space for.

So, let's stop this toxic habit of comparing and making ourselves feel inferior. Let's start developing an awareness of what is real, and what is not.

A powerful perspective on this is to figure out what is NOT for you, what doesn't come naturally to you, what is not part of your make-up.

When you start figuring out what was not meant for you, life adopts a beautiful simplicity, an increased focus. The path to the mountain-top becomes less crowded and you begin to see only the things you want to see.

Creating real and meaningful experiences and relationships is really the purpose of it all. Live and love with grace.

"In the end, only 3 things matter:

How much you loved,

how gently you lived,

and how gracefully you let go of things not meant for you."

- Buddha

<u>Youme challenge:</u>

· What would really touch you deeply to achieve in this coming year?

· Make a mini bucket-list of things that would really have meaning if you could achieve them.

· For each one, make sure you can clearly state a powerful "why" you want to do it.

Then get planning...

WHAT IS NOT FOR ME ?

CHAPTER THIRTEEN:

UNDERSTAND WHAT IS HOLDING YOU BACK

Youme asks: "What do you need to say goodbye to?"

What is there that is taking your time and energy away from growing and progressing?

What things are you hanging on to from the past? Wounds from previous parts of your life still turning up to haunt and hurt you. Even habits and routines that have wiggled their way into our lives and taken root.

And before we know it, these unwanted visitors are camping in our world, draining time and energy, keeping us busy and distracted from seeing the opportunity and relishing the challenges. In the process we are blocked from the headspace to think and dream big.

So, what is the dark shadow sitting in the back of your mind, taking your precious time and energy away and stopping you growing and advancing towards the 'exceptional you'?

"Sometimes letting things go is an act of far greater power than defending or hanging on."

- Eckhart Tolle

Youme challenge:

· What are the things of the past that are still hanging on to a part of you?

· Think of how great it would feel to leave those things behind.

· Now, say goodbye to them for good.

WHAT IS HOLDING
ME BACK?

CHAPTER FOURTEEN:

BECOME AN EXPERT

Youme challenges you: "What are you doing to push yourself towards being an 'expert'?"

Malcolm Gladwell refers to the theoretical measure of 10,000 hours that it takes to be considered an 'expert' in anything. This is one way to try and measure something which remains hard to quantify.

Now, 10,000 hours sounds like a huge time investment, and it is if you must diligently apply yourself to the task. But as history shows, when we as humans become engaged or have a natural interest in something, this milestone can become seemingly effortless. Before dropping out of university, Bill Gates **chose** to spend his days and nights in the computer lab at Harvard, not because he had visions of becoming a billionaire, but because he just loved computers and pursued his passion with gusto and followed where it led him.

As humans, we are drawn magnetically by our interests. From childhood, our hearts and minds get pulled towards those things that intrigue and engage us. And often the result is that when we take a minute to stop and look around, we discover how far we have travelled on the road towards becoming an expert.

Most people are somewhat of an expert at something ...So, what is your thing?

How have you been investing your time over the years?

What has your unique life experience prepared you for?

What is it that you would choose to spend your life doing if money were no object?

And how are you honing that craft and investing into taking yourself to expert status?

"Never become so much of an expert that you stop gaining expertise. View life as a continuous learning experience."

– Denis Waitley

Youme challenge:

Start defining the areas where you have accumulated expertise:

· List what it is you are good at?

· List what it is that you are passionate about?

· List what you do or can provide that people need?

· Deduce what you can make a career or side-career out of?

· Now, start plotting how far you are on the road to becoming an expert in that.

BECOME AN EXPERT

CHAPTER FIFTEEN:

NO ONE GETS TO DEFINE YOU EXCEPT YOU

Youme says: "Only you get to decide what defines you."

The biggest trap we fall into is allowing ourselves to be defined by what we do or have done. Often, we attach our identity (and that of others) to our job, our race, our appearance, our circumstance, how we handled a situation, a specific event.

The job you didn't get. The penalty you missed. That time you behaved badly...or said the wrong thing. These details are just isolated pixels on the big screen of your life.

YOU (and only you) get to define who you are. You know what you are about and what value and goodness you bring to the world.

Start to realise you are not defined by your circumstances, you are defined by your consistent and repeated actions. Life is not a sprint that is over in a few seconds of frenzy. Life is a marathon made up of thousands of decisions and action linked together by your thread.

Measure yourself over the long term on how you have grown and what value you have added. Take pride in laying down each stone in building your legacy.

"We are what we repeatedly do. Success is not an action, but a habit."

- Aristotle

Youme challenge:

You get to define yourself every day, not by words or thoughts, but by the impact you make on the world and the people you interact with, through a consistent series of actions.

· As a gift to yourself, write down a refreshed biography for you (useful to update your social media and other profiles.)

· Try this format:

"I am (describe who you are) …who values (describe what you value) …and who wants to (define the impact you want to have on the world)."

THIS DOES NOT DEFINE
ME

A summary of Youme's lessons

1. Go with The Heart
2. Just Be Yourself
3. Get Out of Your Own Way
4. Decide What You Are Living For
5. Define What You Are Trying to Create
6. Know Who You Need to Be
7. Understand Your Personal Power
8. Manage Your Self-talk
9. Run Your Own Race
10. Getting Your Problems into Perspective
11. Get to The Root of The Problem
12. Decide What Is NOT for You
13. Understand What Is Holding You Back
14. Become an Expert
15. No One Gets to Define You, Except you

Now, rise up and make it ALL POSSIBLE for you.

You have the heart of a lion inside you.

"The greatest fear in the world is the opinion of others. And the moment you are unafraid of the crowd you are no longer a sheep. You become a lion.

A great roar arises in your heart. The roar of freedom."

- Osho

Acknowledgements

I would like to acknowledge several people who have been parts of my journey to this point.

To my soulmate and life partner who reminds me of my song when I forget it.

To my parents who have given all there is to give and have taught me so much about love and life.

To my beautiful children who are my greatest teachers.

To my family and extended family who have and continue to support and mould me.

To my friends who have provided strength and joy sharing the many walkways to this point.

To my many mentors who have helped me to think about how to think, how to do and how to be...Johnny, Ann, Brett, Vlad, Stu, Phil, Jean, Louis, Ernie, Mark, Matthias, Owen to name a few.

To all my coaching clients who have shared their personal journeys with me, and in doing so have allowed me to follow my passion for coaching.

To my friends who have helped me put this work together. To Sami for agreeing to share his talent on illustrating the project. And to Madg for being 'volun-told' to help with the editing.

Here's to you.

About The Author

Duncan Woods (MBA, CPCC) is a certified professional performance coach, author and speaker.

Duncan lives out his passion through coaching clients from all walks of life towards reaching their fill potential, enhancing team cohesion by delivering team workshops, and spreading his messages of personal empowerment as a speaker.

Duncan has spent over 20 years of intensive team and individual coaching in the sporting space, as an international sportsman, captain and coach. He has balanced this with a successful business career with 15 years as a marketer of some respected international brands, whilst also furthering his skills and knowledge culminating in a Masters degree in Business Administration. But most importantly he lists his primary calling as remaining a committed husband and father of three sons.

Through his endeavors he has developed a balanced perspective on career, education, sport, family and combining all of them in pursuit of a successful and fulfilling life with a sense of purpose.

For almost his entire adult life he has been fascinated with the philosophy of personal development, and has spent countless hours working on his own personal outlook on life and the reality that has manifested.

Made in the USA
Middletown, DE
11 January 2019